Cognitive Soccer Passing Patterns & Exercises
Developing Players Technical Ability, Problem Solving Skills & Soccer IQ

By Marcus DiBernardo

Table of Contents

1) Two Group Diamond Rhythm Passing
2) Multiple Choice Passing - Part I
3) Multiple Choice Passing - Part II
4) Pass and Move to Open Cone
5) Problem Solving Passing
6) Passing Using External Cueing
7) Diamond Forward Passing – Part I
8) Diamond Forward Passing – Part II
9) Circle Cognitive Passing
10) Cognitive Circle Combination Passing Using External Cueing
11) Two Patterns – One Time
12) Cognitive Soccer Tennis
13) Moving Triangle
14) Cognitive Star Passing Pattern
15) 3 Ball Cognitive Passing
16) 2 Ball Cognitive Passing
17) Defender Toss Cognitive Passing
18) 4v1 Rondo Partner Passing
19) Elastic Band Passing Pattern
20) Hat Color Passing Exercise

Cognitive Soccer Passing Patterns & Exercises

The idea of cognitive soccer training is to develop the players' ability to process information, so they can effectively problem solve and find soccer solutions on the field. When a training exercise is becoming too easy add another layer of complexity to the drill. Also, when training cognitive soccer exercises it is important to keep changing drills day after day and week after week. The more unique experiences players can experience the better. The variations in exercises will help increase the player's ability to process information while building their internal grid (soccer memory & IQ). Cognitive soccer training can use varying numbers of players, multiple sized grids, various rules & conditions, different field surfaces and different sized balls. All of these potential variations will add levels of complexity to the exercises, forcing players to find solutions to the new conditions in order to be effective. These various training experiences are all very important in the process of developing "Soccer Intelligence or Soccer IQ".

Enjoy the book and please feel free to email any feedback to me at coachdibernardo@gmail.com

Exercise One

Two Group Diamond Rhythm Passing

Players: 8 Players

Grid: 30x30 yards (split to make 2 grids of 30x15)

Instructions and Key Points:
Each group of four has a ball and forms a basic diamond shape to start. Players in the diamond can move to the center, overlap or exchange with another player during passing. However, there should always be a minimum of a triangle shape present. After five passes the group will transition the ball to the opposite grid & group. It is very important that both groups remain in rhythm with each other. When a group is ready to switch the ball to the other side, the player on the ball can take 2-touches and pick out a player to pass to. **Variations & Building Complexity:** all switched balls must be played in the air, play a required pattern of 2-touch followed by 1-touch, color-code the players (two red and two blue in each group) requiring players not to play to the same color. By adding more conditions and rules the players will be forced to problem solve.

Two group Diamond Rhythm Passing:

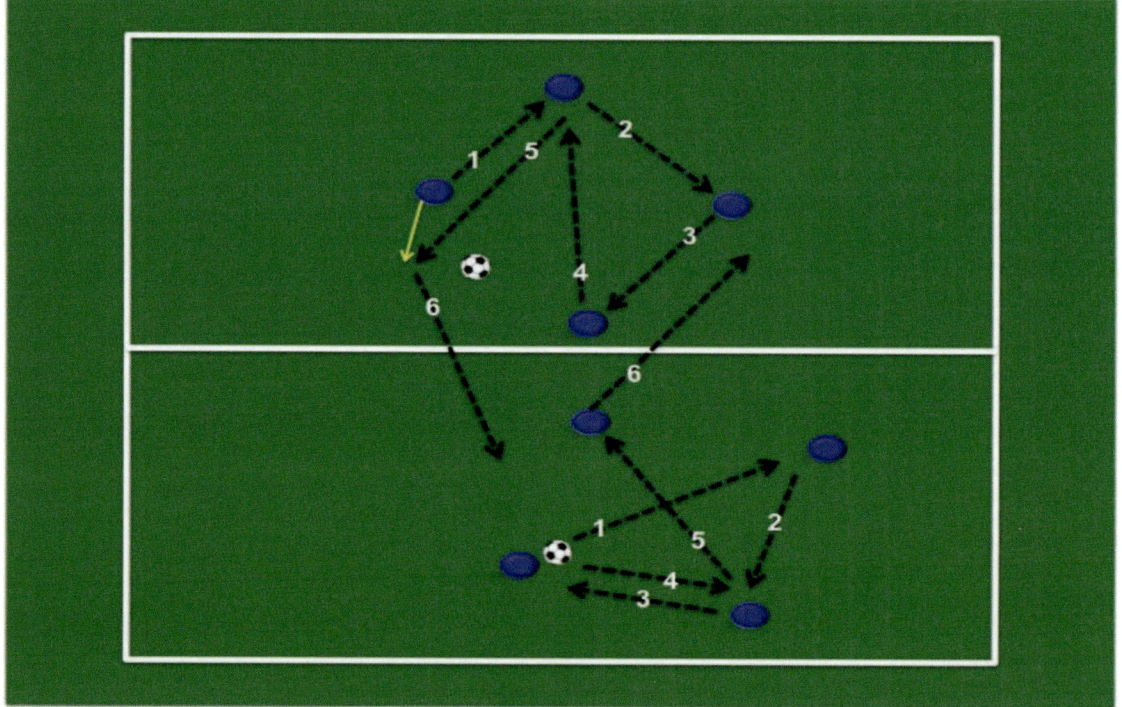

Exercise Two & Three

Multiple Choice Passing

Players: 12 Players

Grid: 35x30 yards

Instructions and Key Points:
The red players must pass to blue and blue to red. Players move off their cone a couple of feet to receive the ball once eye contact is made with the passing player. Firm passing and eye contact between passer and receiver are essential.
Variations & Building Complexity: Increase number of balls to 3, encourage 1-touch passing, have players follow their pass and take up the position on the new cone, each player has a tennis ball they must bounce and catch before passing the soccer ball.

Multiple Choice Passing:

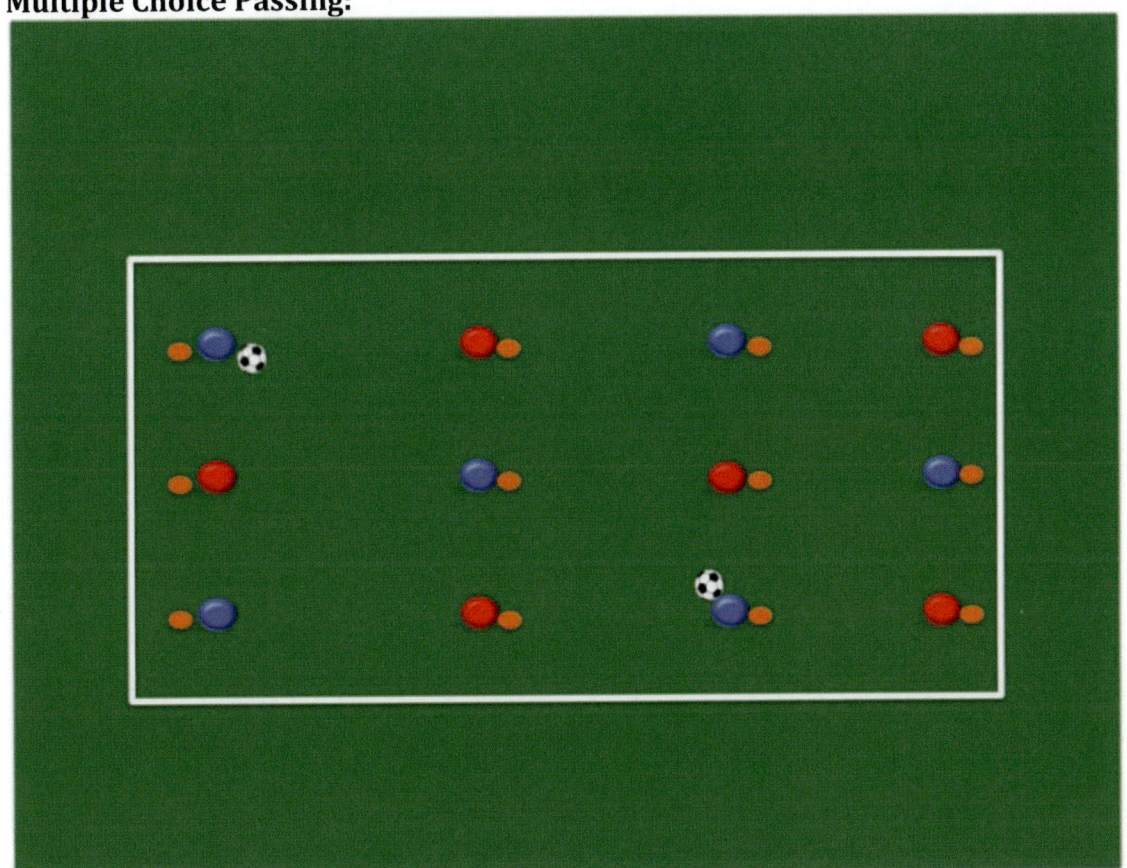

Multiple Choice Passing:
This variation requires red to play to yellow, yellow to blue and blue to red. The same variations from the previous drill can be applied to add complexity.

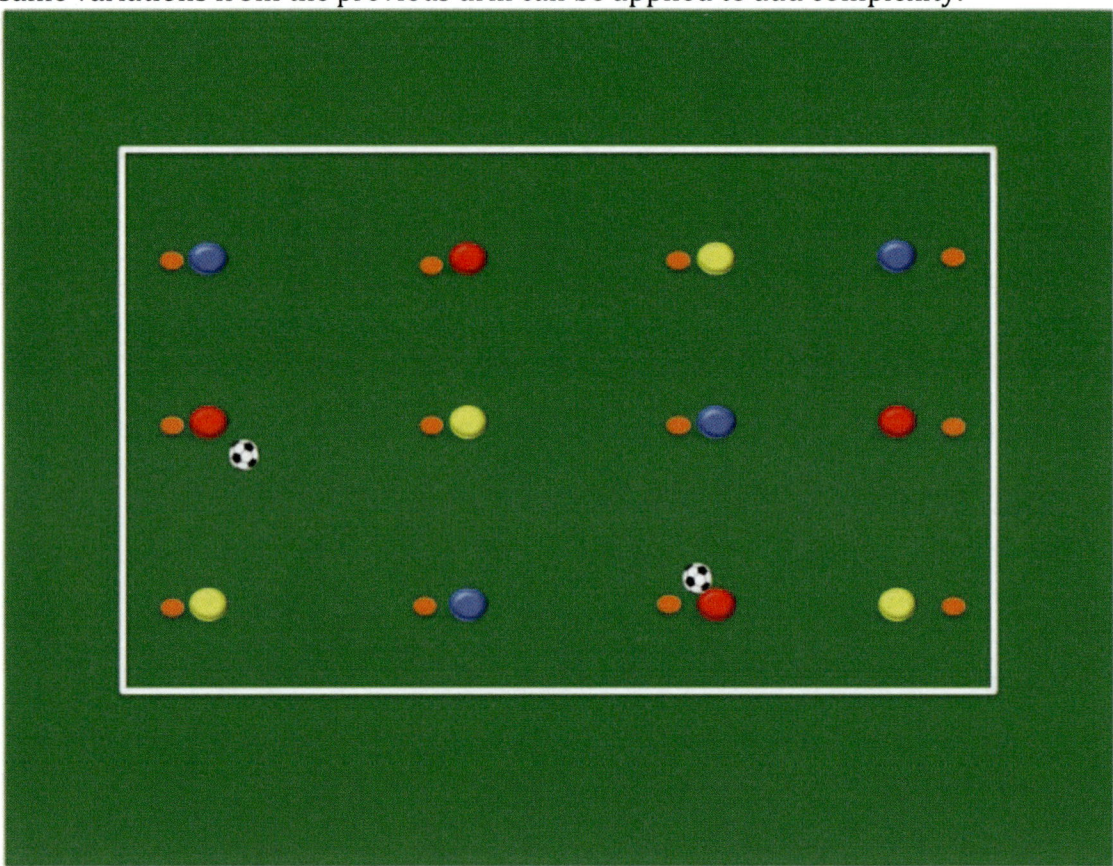

Exercise Four

Pass and Move to Empty Cone

Players: 6-12 Players
Grid: 20x30 yards
Instructions and Key Points:
The players on the ball must make eye contact with any free player and pass the ball to that player. After making the pass, the player who passed the ball must sprint to any empty cone. Play 2-touch and insist the tempo stays high. The exercise is more difficult than it looks. Variations & Building Complexity: The more balls added the more difficult the exercise becomes, build the balls to the point that half the players have a ball. Make the cones 5 different colors, and shout a color out, which means no player can run to that color cone. Add the rule that the player the pass is played into, must 1-touch the ball back to the passer, who 1-touches it back and runs to an empty cone. Using variations and building overloads will make this game into a cognitive activity that is very demanding.

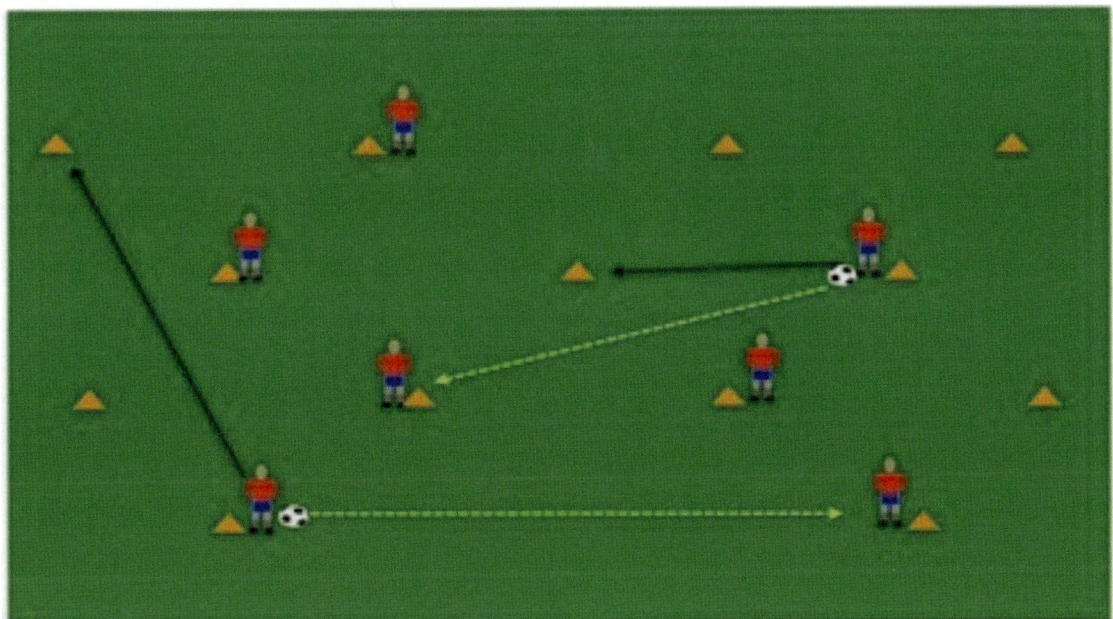

Exercise Five

Problem Solving Passing

Players: 4 Players
Grid: Diamond
Instructions and Key Points:
The player passes directly across the grid and then chooses a side to run to, as all three players must take up a new spot, the only player not moving is the player who received the ball. Once the players have taken up their new positions, the player on the ball will pass it back across and the pattern continues. You will notice the exercise is not easy, as players will need to communicate with each other get to the correct spot quickly. Variations & Building Complexity: Have the passing player follow the pass into the middle and receive a 1-touch pass back, play it back 1-touch and then choose a side to run to from the middle.

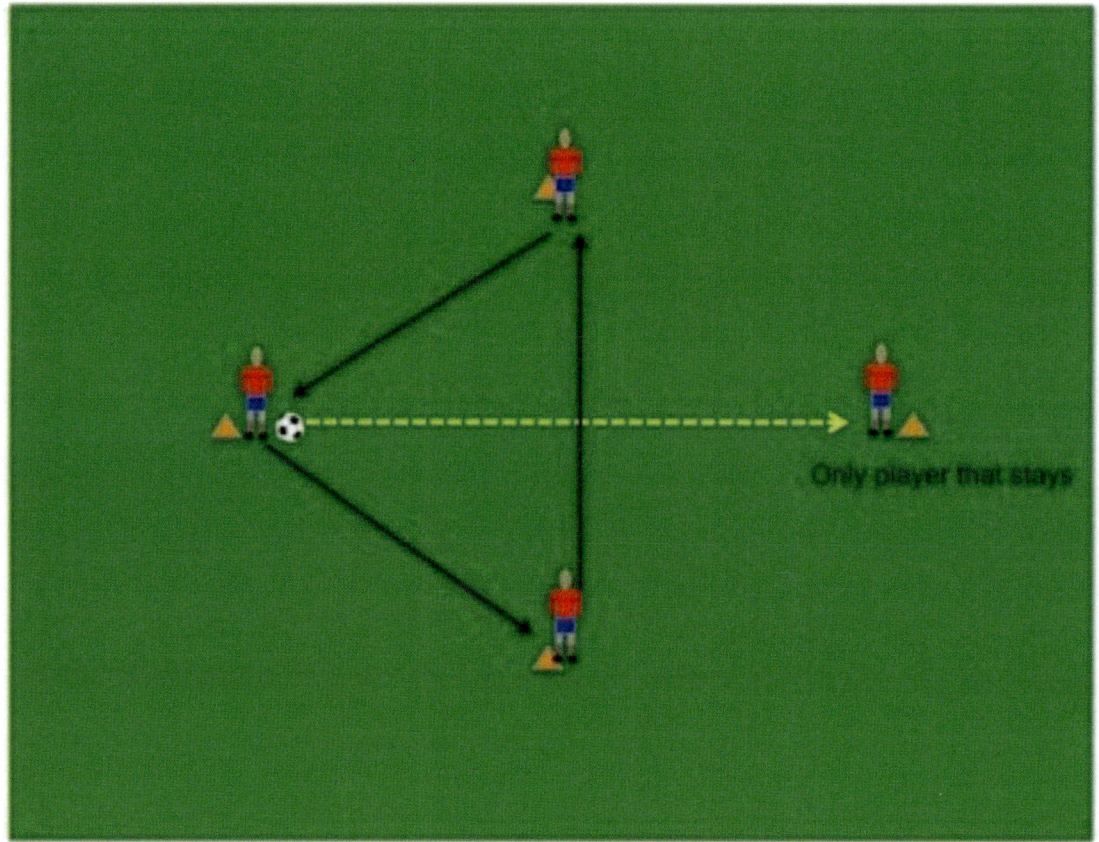

Exercise Six

Passing using External Cueing

Players: 8 Players
Grid: 20 x 20 yards
Instructions and Key Points:
The red circles are speed rings that are used as a cue for players to step in and out of to receive the pass, the blue cones serve as gates that the ball must be played through, these blue cones serve as external cues. **Variations & Building Complexity:** Have the players wear different color bibs, as the receiving players and passing player must shout out what color bib they are receiving the ball from and passing the ball to.

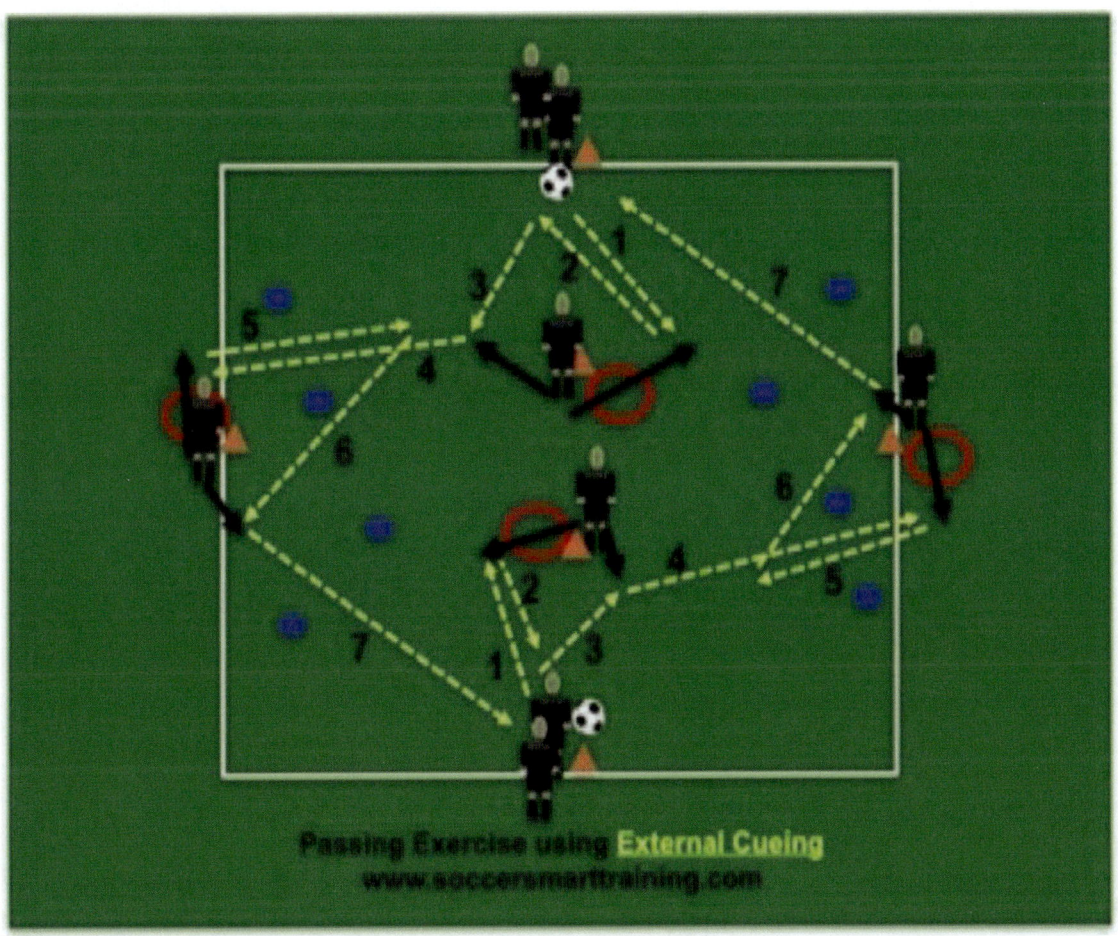

Passing Exercise using External Cueing
www.soccersmarttraining.com

Exercise Seven & Eight

Diamond Forward Passing

Players: 5 Players

Grid: 20x40 yards (split to make 2 grids of 20x20 yards)

Instructions and Key Points:
Four players form a diamond or triangle playing 1-touch. Players can interchange positions and have movement while forming the diamond or triangle. After 4 or more passes the ball will be played into the opposite grid to the target player. Three players will follow the pass into the grid to form another diamond. The player who played the ball in must follow the pass into the next grid. This will encourage forward passing and running. **Variations & Building Complexity:** the ball played into the target must be in the air, all passes must be in the air with only once bounce allowed between passing, ball can only be played forward to the next grid by the deepest player.

Diamond Forward Passing Part I:

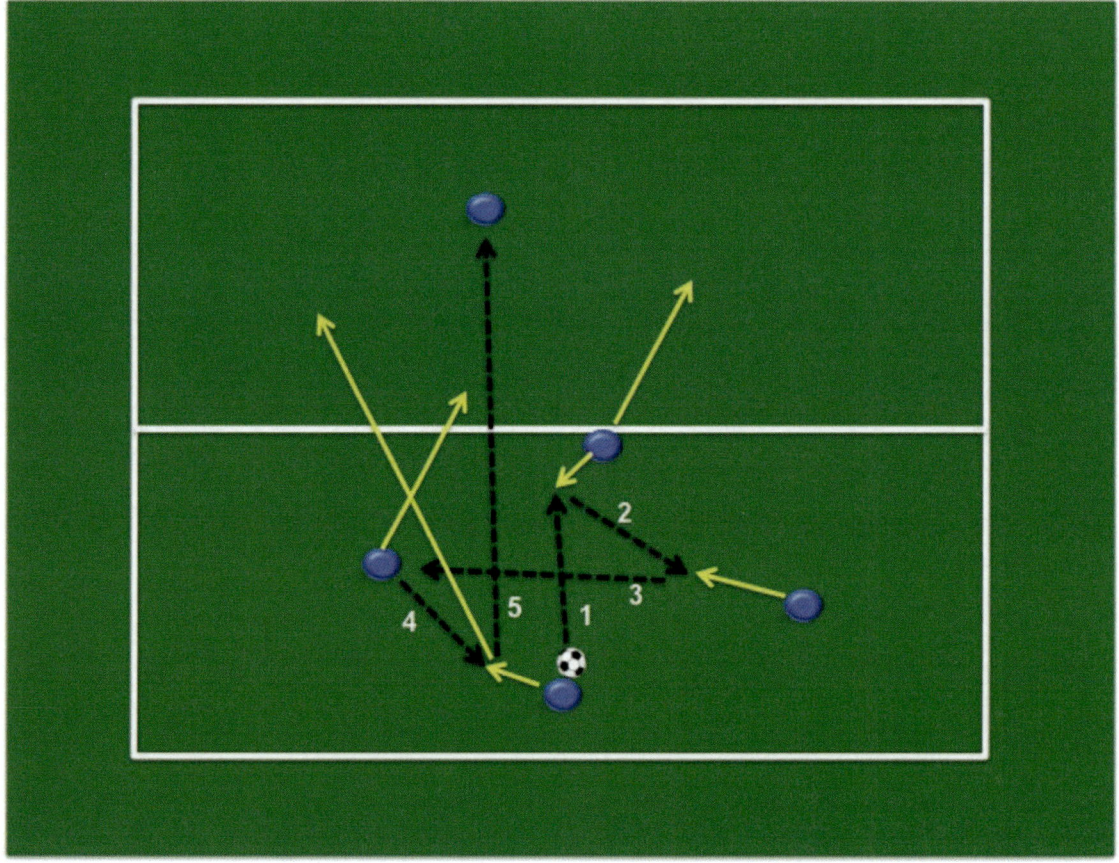

Diamond Forward Passing Part II: Grid (40x40 yards)

This exercise will be the same as Part I but the passer will choose the free target player to play into. Each group must be very aware of the other group and what target player they are playing into.

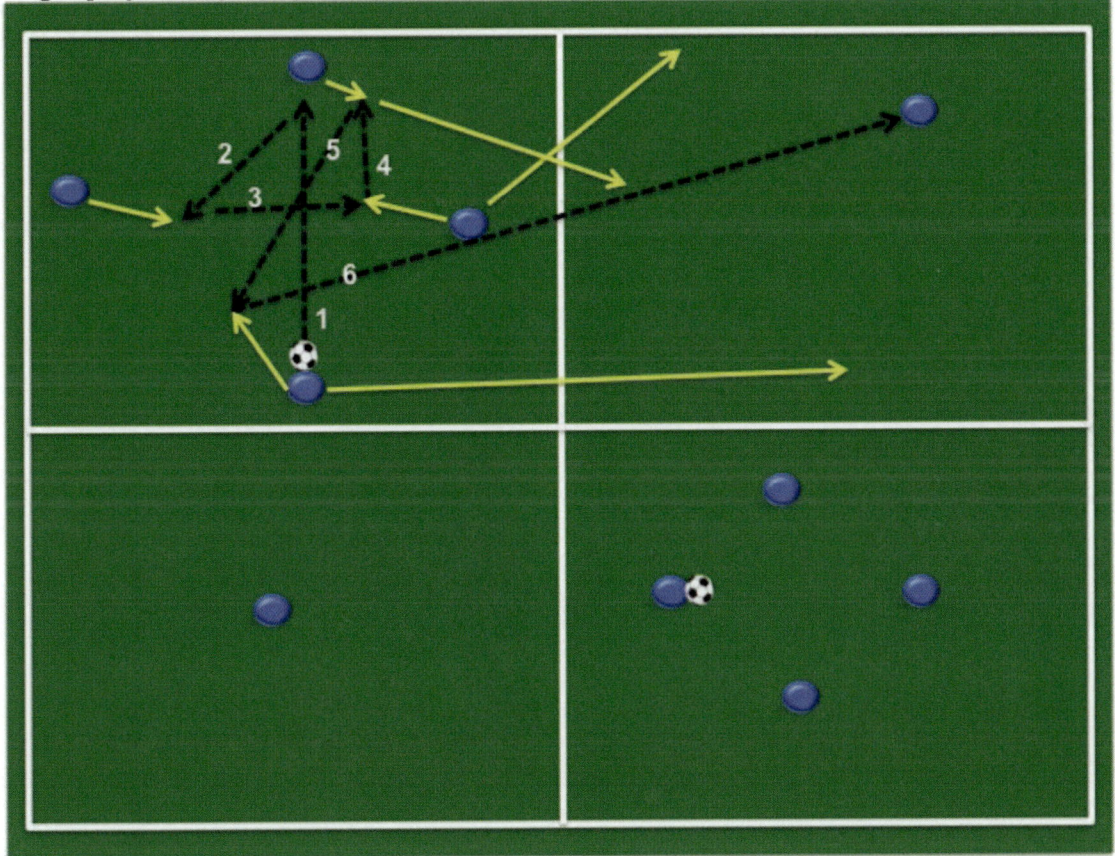

Exercise Nine

Circle Cognitive Passing

Players: 8-14 Players

Grid: 15X15 yards in a circle

Instructions and Key Points:
Start with one soccer ball on the ground playing 1-touch and another ball held in a players hands. In the diagram the ball in the players hands is in black. The players toss 1 ball under hand to each other as the ball on the ground is passed 1-touch. Players must open their vision to enable them to see both balls at once. The exercise can take up to 14 players. **Variations & Building Complexity:** 2 balls being played on the ground 1-touch & 1 in the air, 2 balls in the air being tossed and 1 ball on the ground 1-touch, 2 balls being tossed in the air and 2 balls being passed 1-touch on the ground. The players can also be split into red & blue – players would not be allowed to play to the same color. Change the rule so players toss the ball to same color but 1-touch ground pass must be to the opposite color. The complexity of this drill can become very challenging as the layers are built.

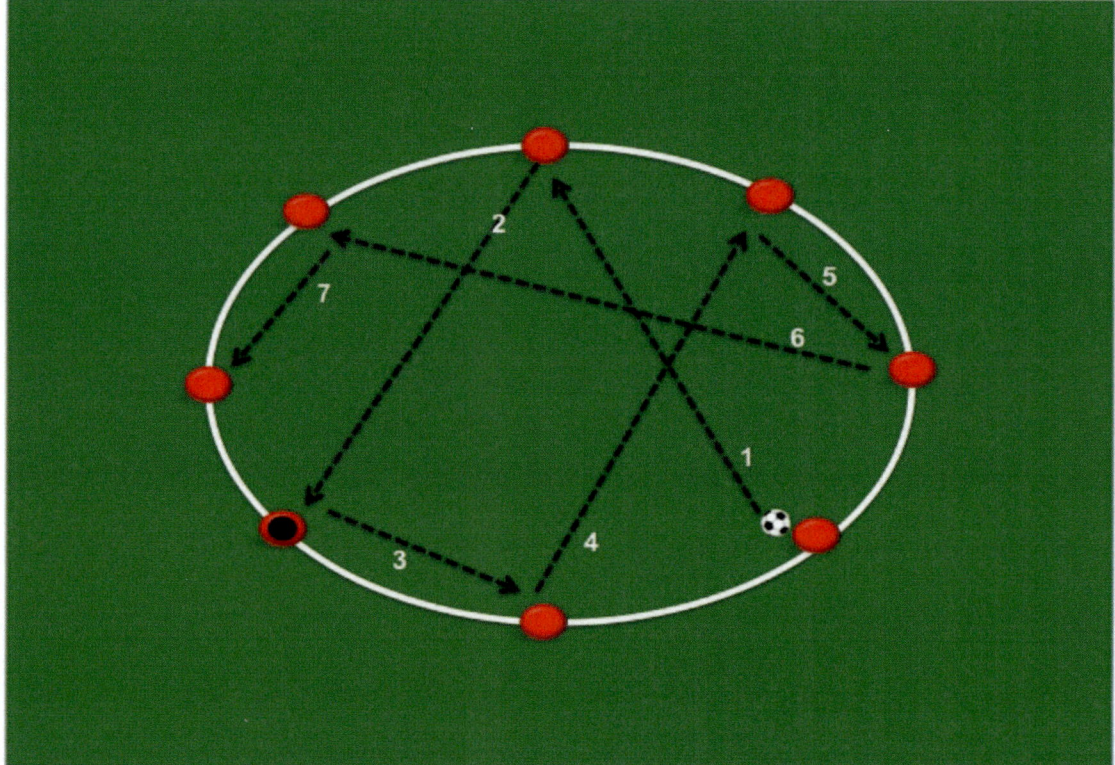

Exercise Ten

Cognitive Circle Combination Passing Using External Cueing

Players: 4 groups of 2 players each (8 players total)
Grid: 15x15 yard circle
Instructions & Key Points:
This exercise can be played 1 or 2 touch and uses the cones as external cues to determine if the pass was successful or not. In this example, the player with the ball passes into the yellow player who 1-touches the ball back to the passer who has now run into the center of the circle, the player will now pass through any gate to a new player and take their position on the outside of the circle. The new player in possession of the ball outside the circle can take 2-touches and then play to another person through the circle as the pattern continues. To add complexity do not allow players to pass to their partners, use different size balls or make every pass 1-touch.

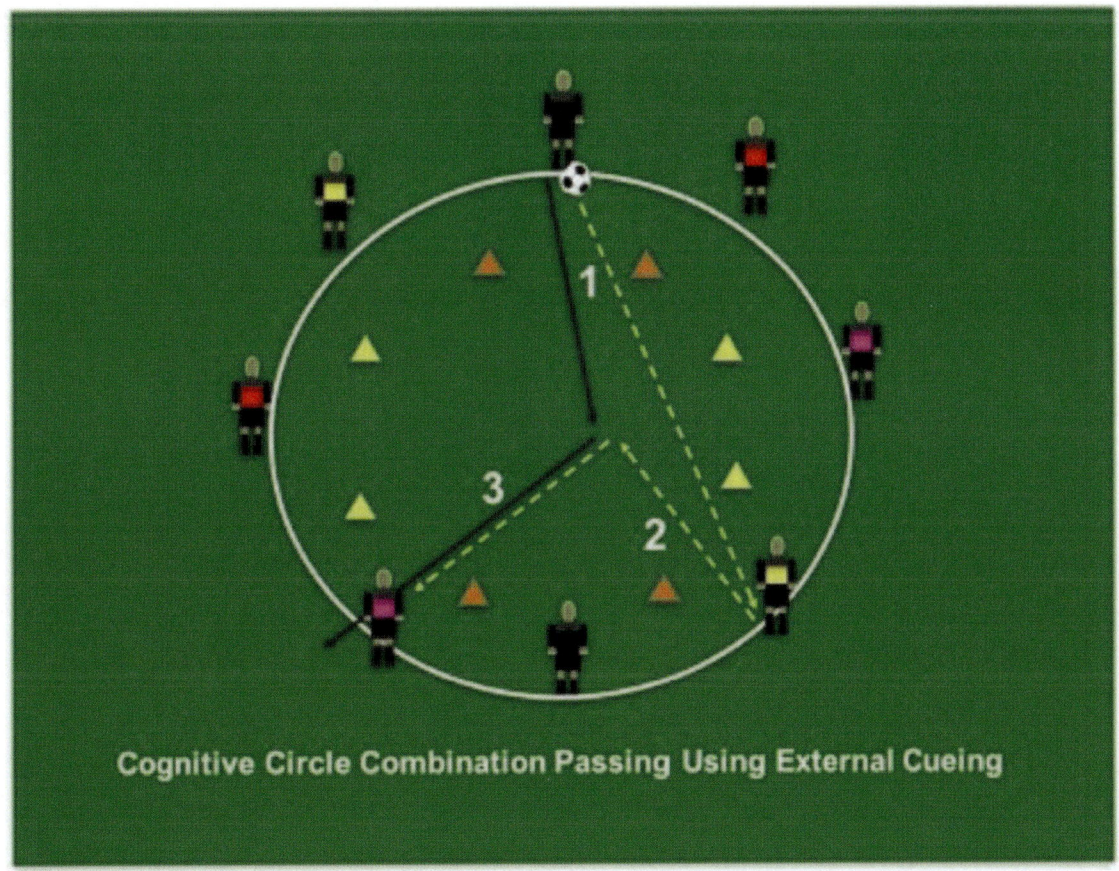

Cognitive Circle Combination Passing Using External Cueing

Exercise Eleven

Two Patterns – One Time

Players: 12-18 Players

Grid: 40x40 Yard Grid

Instructions and Key Points:
There are two separate passing patterns happening at the same time. When the patterns intersect the timing of player's runs, weight of the passes, coordination of movements and player vision must be perfect. The confusion of multiple runs and balls being played in all directions forces players to concentrate and process multiple streams of information. The pattern should be done 2-touch, inside of foot control and inside of foot passing. **Variations & Building Complexity:** Have players in various color vests - they must shout out the color of the player passing them the ball and the color of the person they will be passing to, place a circular ring (shown in black) on the ground to the side and slightly behind the cone – have the receiving player glance over their shoulder and step one foot into the ring and than pop back out ready to receive the pass – the glance over the shoulder while stepping into the ring helps players to scan the field before receiving the ball and adds another layer of information to the pattern.

Two Patterns – One Time:

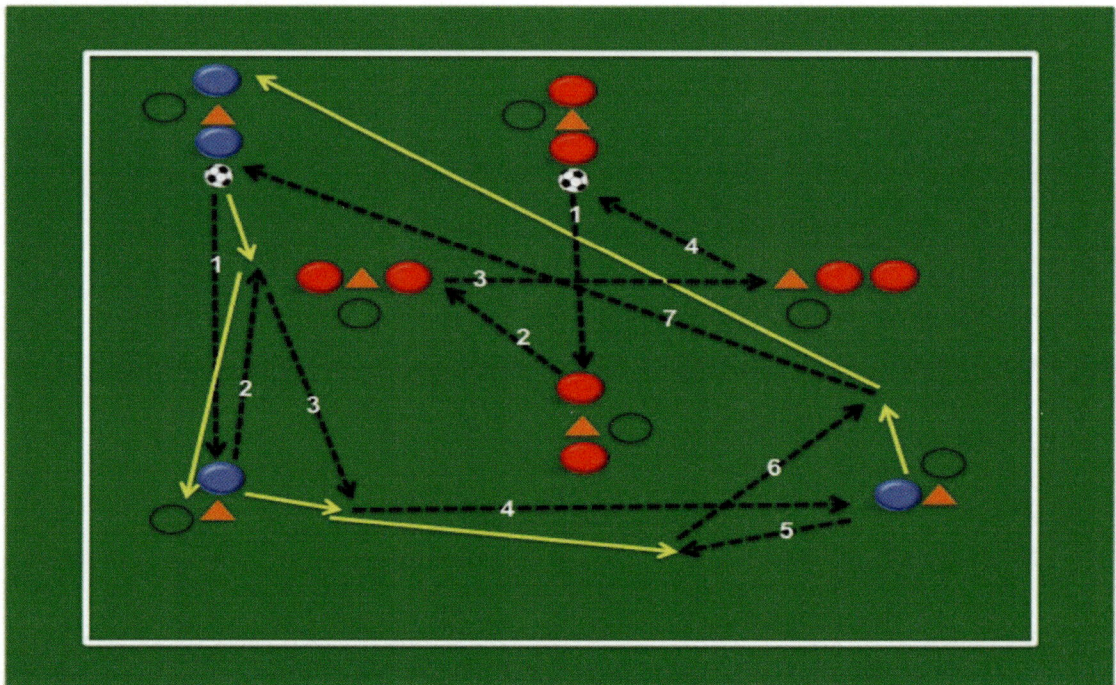

Exercise Twelve

Cognitive Soccer Tennis

Players: 8 Players

Grid: 15x30 yards (split to make 2 grids of 15x15)

Instructions and Key Points:
This game is played with a small net or marked with cones. If cones are used as the net, the pass into the opposite grid must be above knee height and no spiking! Players must only pass to the opposite color player on their team while playing 1-touch in the air only. Lower skill levels can be allowed one bounce. **Variations & Building Complexity:** only feet and head touches, only chest and feet touches, only thigh and feet, allow 2-touches but every player on the team must touch the ball before playing across.

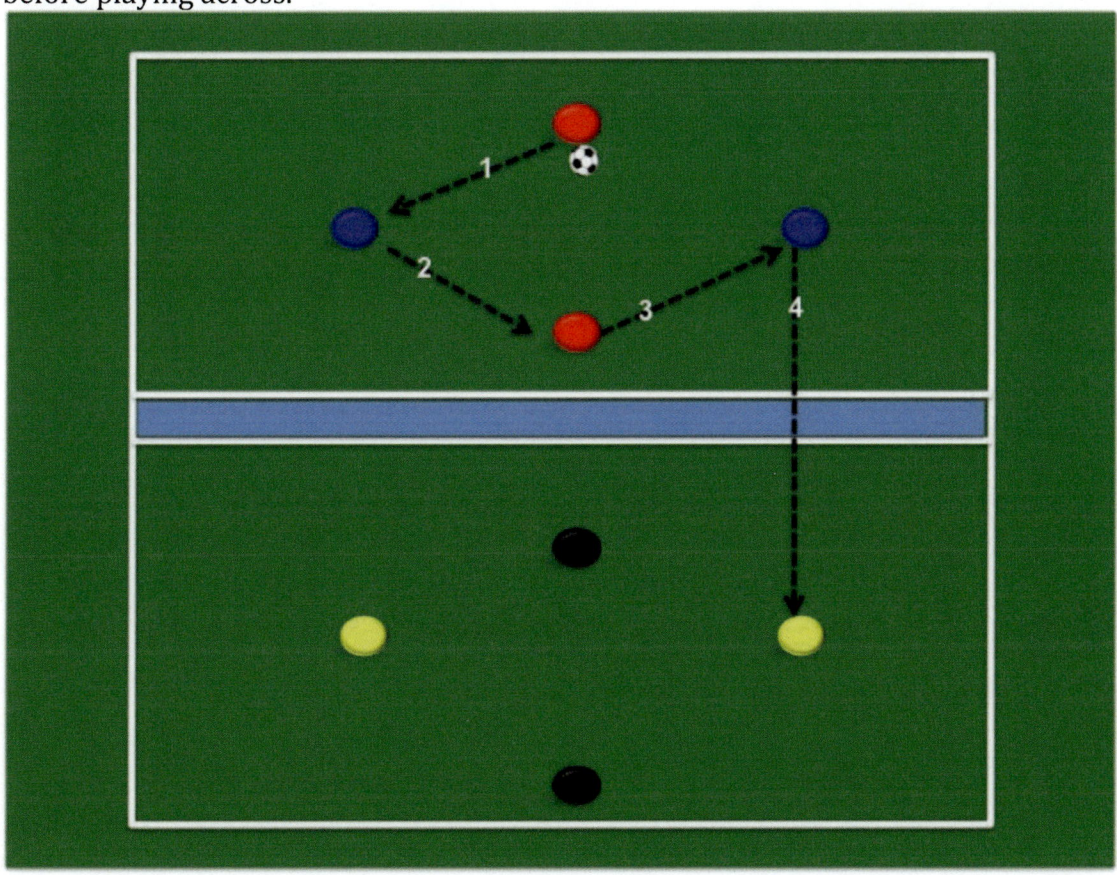

Exercise Thirteen

Moving Triangle

Players: 4 Players

Grid: 30x30 yards (split to make 2 grids of 15x30)

Instructions and Key Points:
Players in the triangle must make a minimum of 3 passes before playing a forward ball into the next grid. Two players will release when the ball is played to the target. The basic triangle shape should be kept in passing possession.

Variations & Building Complexity: the player playing into the target must follow the pass to encourage forward passing and running, the ball played in must be in the air, the target player can be moving inside the grid.

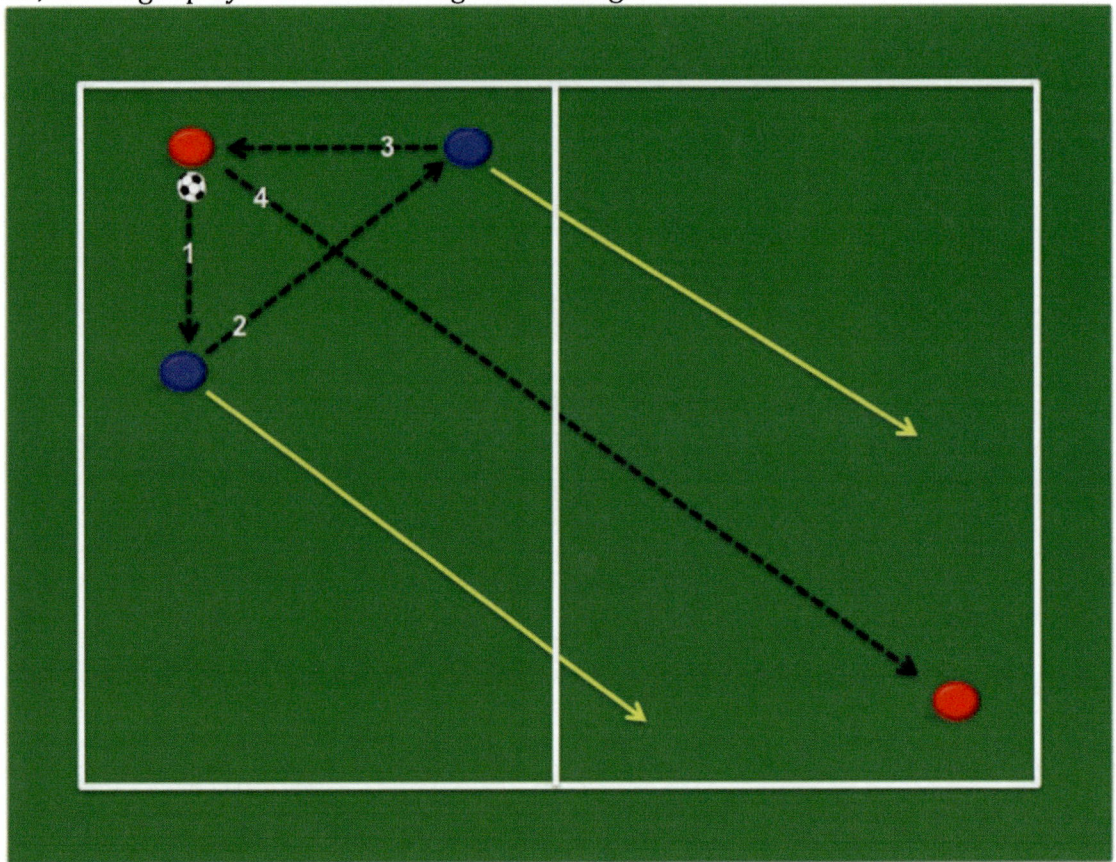

Exercise Fourteen

Cognitive Star Passing Pattern

Players: 16 Players

Grid: Can set at various distances depending on length of passing desired

Instructions and key Points:

Start with one ball. If the group does well, work in a second ball and third ball. The first player in each line will have a tennis ball in their hand, including the passer. The player receiving the soccer ball pass must pop off the cone about a foot, presenting a good target for the passing player. It is very important that there is coordinated movement, synchronization and rhythm between the passer and receiver. Insist the passer make eye contact with the receiver before the pass is made. The first cognitive challenge for the receiving player will be to turn quickly before receiving the soccer ball pass and toss the tennis ball back to the player standing behind him in line. The receiving player is forced to get check over his shoulder before receiving a pass. **Variations & Building Complexity:** make the tennis ball toss a bounce pass requiring more coordination and timing. Each player will wear a color-training vest. Mix up the vests/bibs with at least four to five different colors. The next progression is to have the receiving soccer pass player call out the color of the bib of the player they passed the tennis ball to, then call out the color of the bib of the player who passed them the soccer ball and finally call out the color of the new player who they are passing the soccer ball to. Build the drill from simple to complex. Start with just the passing pattern and then add in all the cognitive rules and conditions one at a time. This will create the overload that will challenge the players.

This passing pattern is no longer a simple repetitive drill when you add the cognitive dimension to it. The drill has been transformed into a challenging cognitive exercise that works the brain as well as soccer passing technique. Once all the cognitive progressions are accomplished have the players do the drill just passing the ball and not cognitive demands. You will see how easy the drill will become. I like to do this, so the players can see how much harder the drill was with the cognitive conditions.

Cognitive Star Passing Pattern:

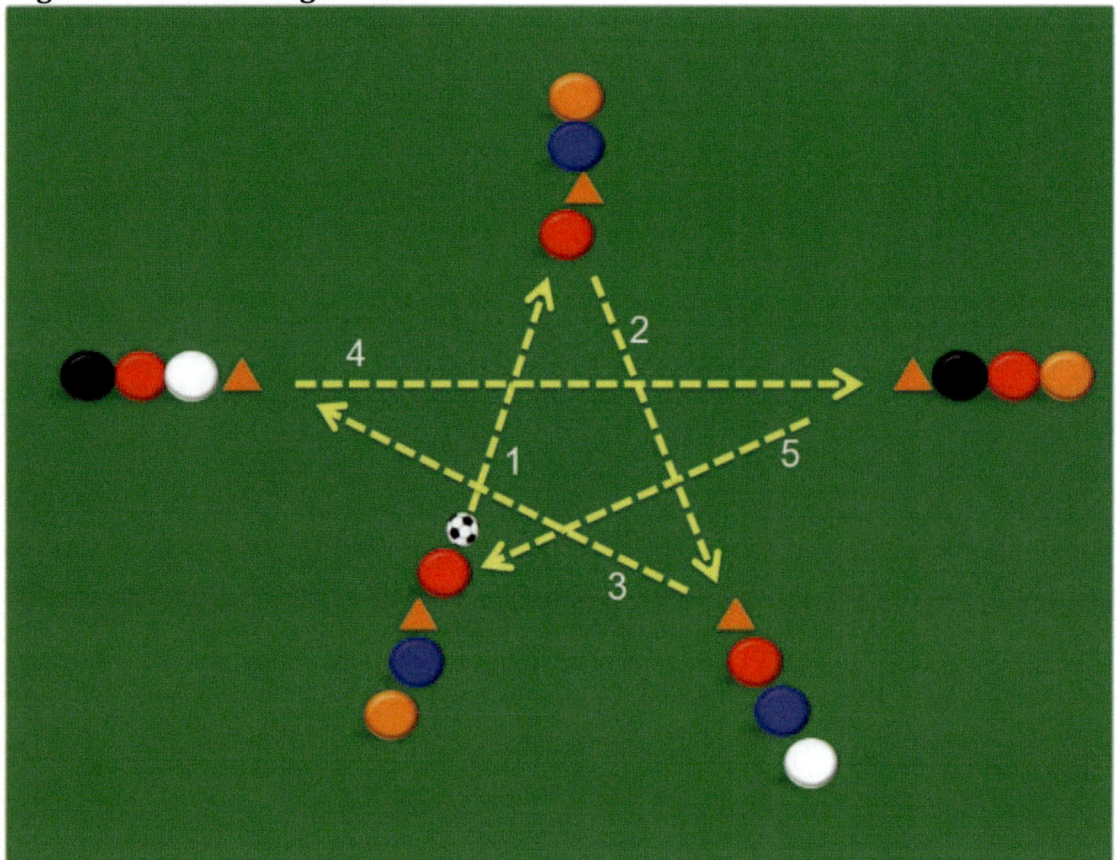

Exercise Fifteen

3 Ball Cognitive Passing

Players: 12 Players
Grid: 25x25 yards
Instructions and Key Points:
In this creative cognitive passing exercise blue must pass to red, red must pass to black and black to blue. Both soccer balls are passed to feet on the ground while another ball (shown in orange held by the red player) is tossed in the same sequence but to the hands. The soccer balls must be played 2-touch. All players must always be moving. This exercise requires players to constantly be processing other player's locations and where the balls are.

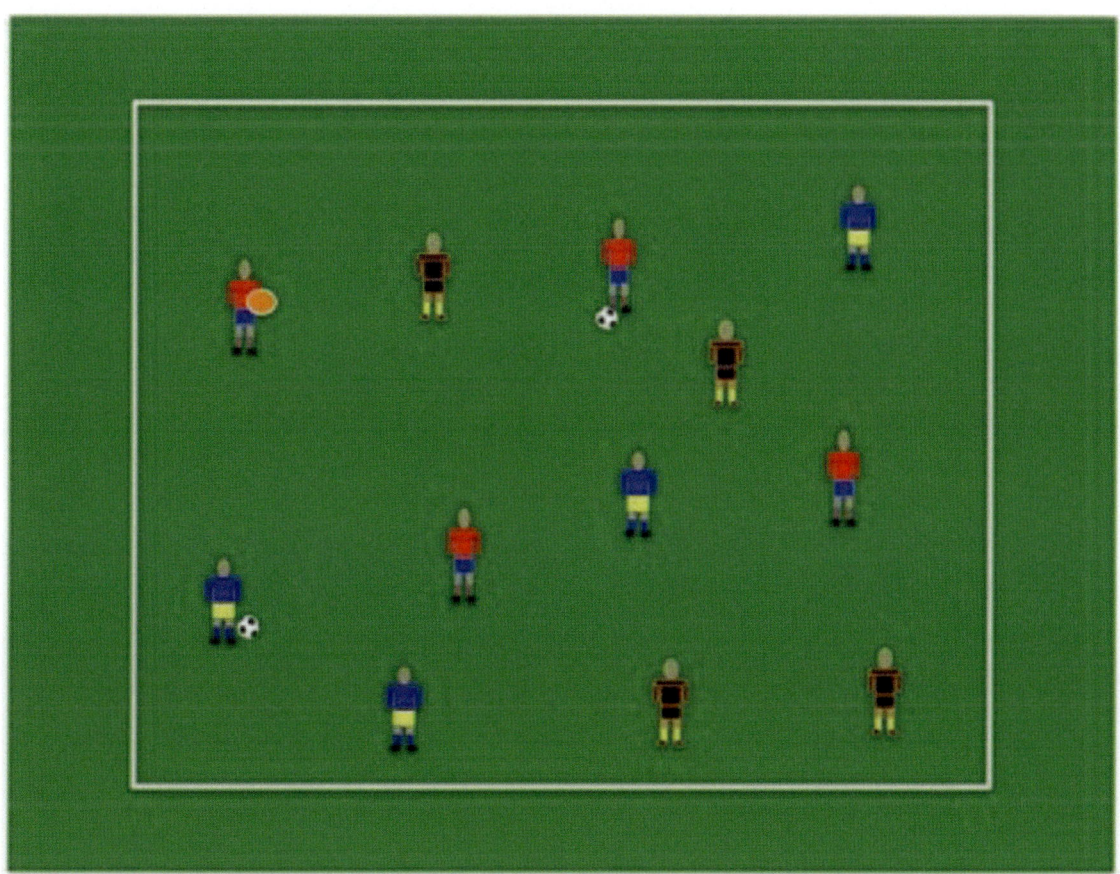

Exercise Sixteen

2 Ball Cognitive Passing

Players: 12 Players
Grid: 25x25 yards
Instructions and Key Points:
The exercise is the same as exercise #15 but the ball that is being tossed to hands is removed. The two soccer balls must be passed in the correct color sequence and 2-touch. One defender is now added to the exercise as well. Now players must process the location of the soccer balls, the location of players and the location of the defender. The end result is players are forced to increase their head movement and the amount of information they take in. We know that players with increased head movement complete more passes and 2/3 more forward passes. The defender can be swapped out every 60-90 seconds. If the defender wins the ball, have him play it back to a free player and play starts again.

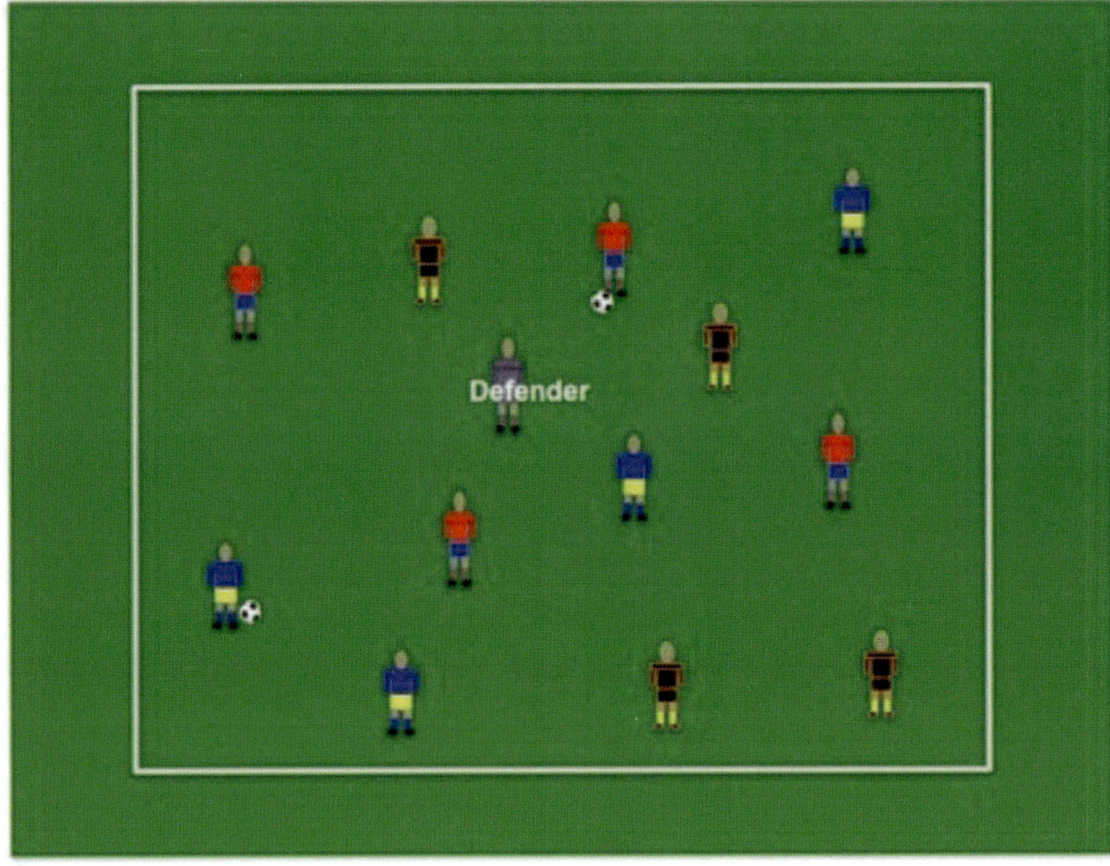

Exercise Seventeen

Defender Ball Toss Cognitive Passing

Players: 12 Players
Grid: 25x25 yards
Instructions and Key Points:

This is last variation of the previous exercise, it allows the defender to have a soft ball that he can throw at any player – if the player is hit they must do 5 quick push-ups or sprint to a cone outside the grid and come back. This variation adds a new dimension of player spacing and knowledge of who is around them. Start with one soccer ball and add another if the group is skilled. Excellent game for spatial awareness and scanning. If the group is larger and technical add two defenders both will balls to throw.

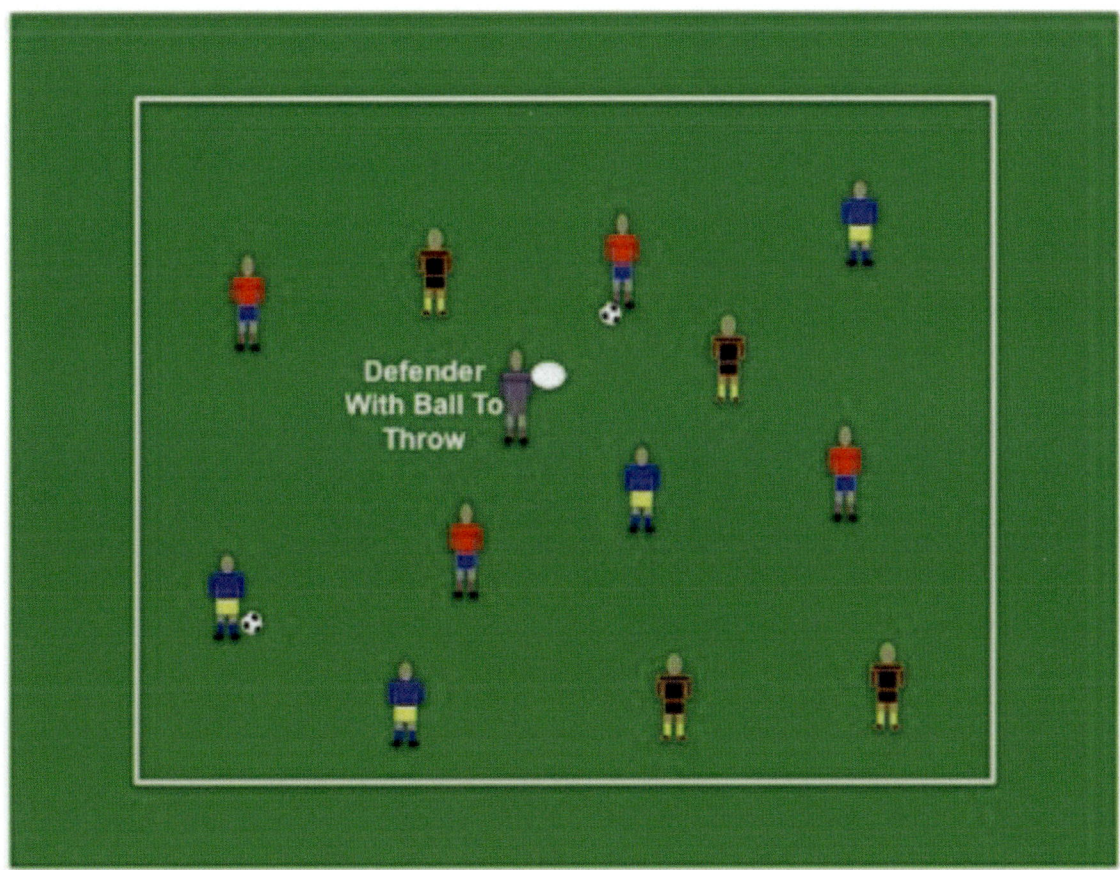

Exercise Eighteen

4v1 Rondo & Partner Passing

Players: 8 Players
Grid: 15x15 Yard Grid
Instructions and Key Points:
The group plays 4v1, 1 or 2 touch, after 4 passes the group can switch the ball to the far end. When the ball is switched, side players travel or slide down into the next square as the middle player simply turns to join the new 4v1. The end player who stays switches positions with the player on his side that is passing 1-touch with a partner. The idea is to get the timing so coordinated that the 1-touch partner passing is never interrupted by the switching, as the end player switches into the passing and the passer switches into the grid. **Variations & Building Complexity:** 1-touch for everyone, partner passers must use only left foot. Add a hurdle that partner passes must chip ball over to partner, or cones that make a gate for ball to be passed through with partner.

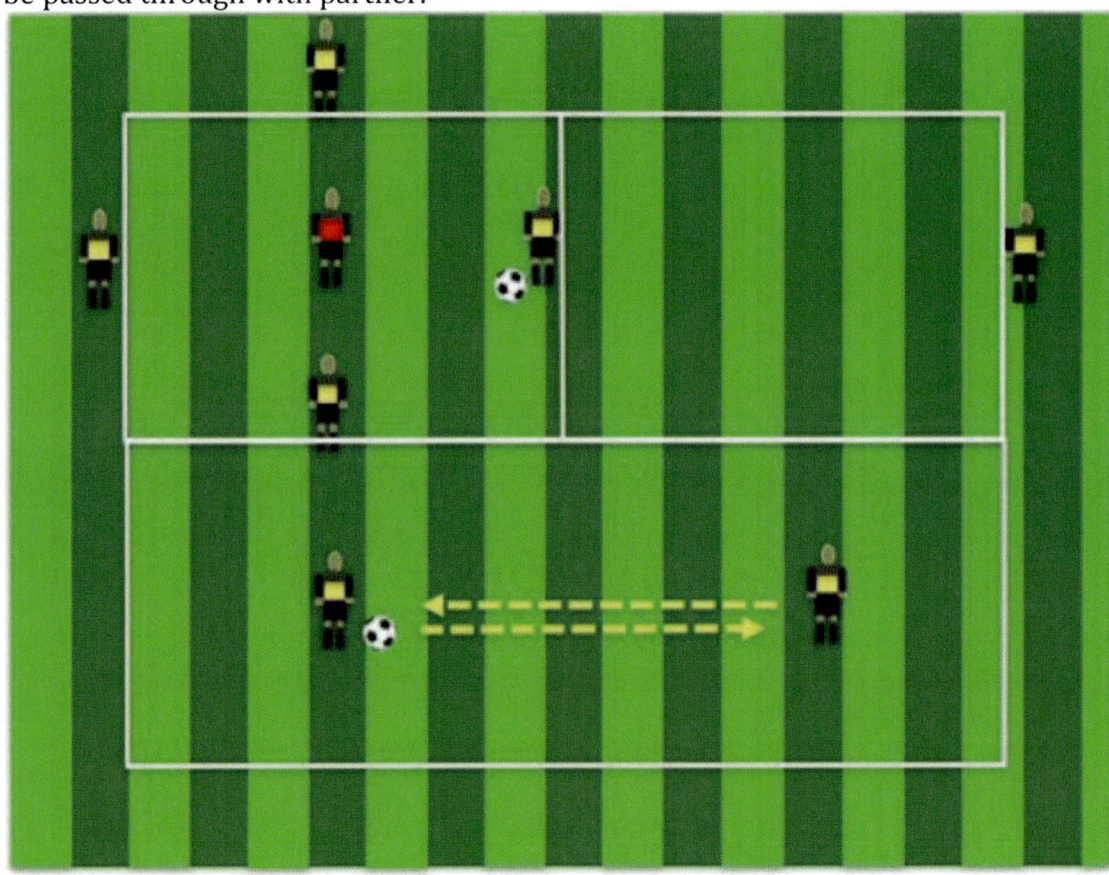

Exercise Nineteen

Elastic Band Passing Pattern

Players: 8 Players

Grid: 15x15 yards

Instructions and Key Points:
Players are required to hold a 12 inch elastic or rope with two hands behind their back when performing the passing pattern. When players are forced to have both hands behind their back it limits their mobility and forces them to concentrate on proper body positioning and individual technique. It is even more important with the decreased mobility that passing be accurate and to the correct foot. Two-touch passing is required - inside of the foot control with inside of foot pass.
Variations & Building Complexity: Change the pattern to 1-touch only.
Elastic Band Passing Pattern:

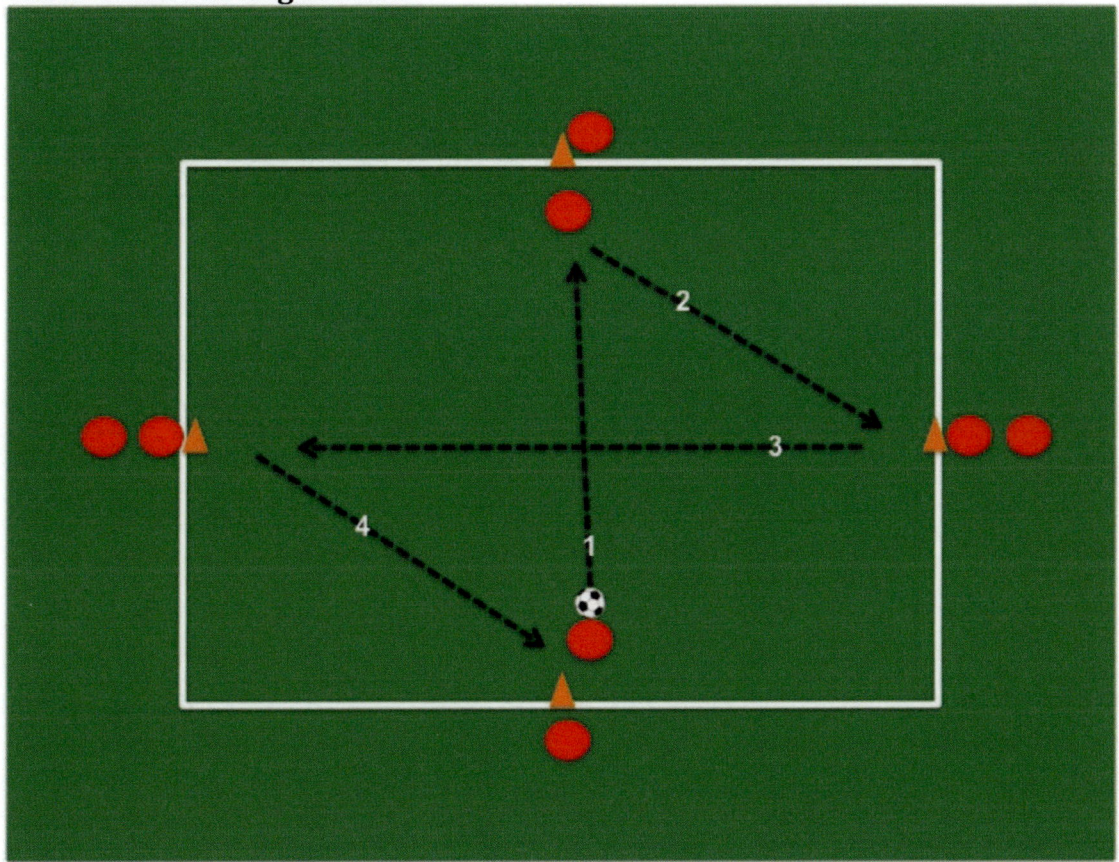

Exercise Twenty

Hat Color Passing Exercise

Players: 12 Players

Grid: 25x25 yards

Instructions and Key Points:
The players are split into 3 groups of 4 players each – blue, yellow & red. Players wear a small hat that will identify their color – try a small party hat. Blue must pass to red, red to yellow and yellow to blue. Players are forced to open up their vision having to identify the hats as the only visual cue. Start the exercise requiring 2-touch with 2 soccer balls. **Variations & Building Complexity:** Play 1-touch, add a 3rd soccer ball, play 2 soccer balls and a 3rd to be tossed in the air to each other in any order while the regular exercise is being carried out.

Hat Color Passing Exercise:

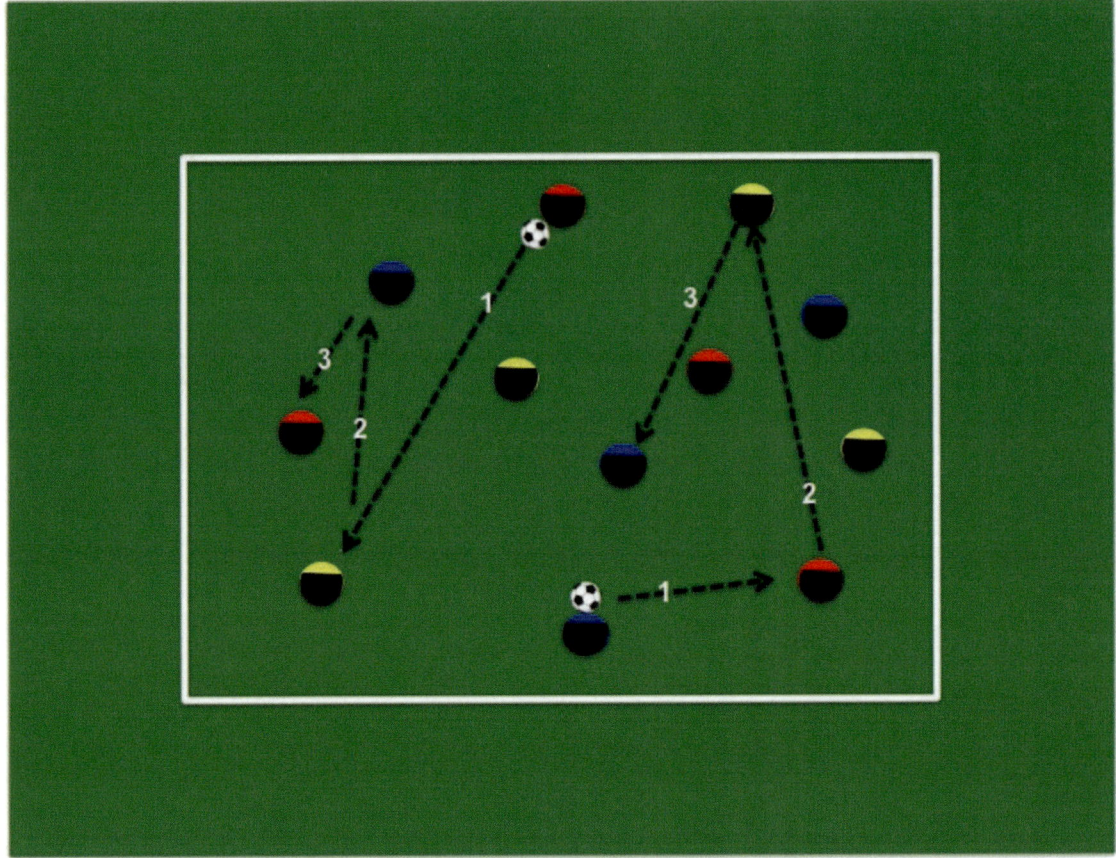

Manufactured by Amazon.ca
Bolton, ON